An opi

CALM
LONDON

Written by
CHRISTINA
ROSE BROWN

Rothko Room, Tate Modern (no.44)

INFORMATION IS DEAD.
LONG LIVE OPINION.

What's the point of a guidebook? A quick Google will throw up millions of calm things to do in London.

But that wouldn't be very calming. When you're craving some peace or space to think, you don't want millions of ideas; you want a short, trustworthy selection of *only* the most relaxing places in the city. Here it is.

Martin
Hoxton Mini Press

Earl of East (no.55)
Opposite: Re:Mind (no.56)

Hampstead Heath (no.18)
Opposite: Isabella Plantation (no.49)

...AND *BREATHE*

It's an oft quoted cliché that 'When a man is tired of London, he is tired of life.' Well, sometimes us Londoners are just plain *tired*. Whether it's spending our Monday morning commute pressed up against a stranger's armpit on the packed Piccadilly line or jostling to get served in the latest pop-up cocktail bar, London life can be pretty full-on. And don't even get me started on trying to navigate Oxford Street on a Saturday afternoon. No wonder we sometimes just want to press pause.

Thankfully, away from the crowds and the traffic and the rush-hour Tube, there is another side to this city. Nestled among the bustling streets are myriad secluded sanctuaries. Did you know that one of the capital's most beautiful (and affordable) spas is hidden under a public swimming pool, moments from Old Street roundabout? That there is a traditional Scandi sauna in the basement of a church in Rotherhithe? Or how about the homely Japanese restaurant where you can eat your dinner wearing slippers?

London's vibrant mix of people, cultures and religions is what makes it such a brilliant city – and means there are an abundance of different ways to find serenity. Take in a classic choral evensong in the majestic surroundings of St Martin-in-the-Fields (no.4) or join a transcendental meditation with robed monks in a temple that looks like it's been teleported straight from the hills of northern Thailand (no.42). If you're after a more New Age brand of spirituality, head to

She's Lost Control (no.35) for crystal therapies, aura readings and tarot workshops, or book a one-on-one session with a modern reiki master (no.22).

But you don't have to be seeking spiritual enlightenment to benefit from this book. Calm isn't just found in London's plentiful yoga studios and meditation classes; it's anywhere in the city that offers space to stop and think, to catch your breath and notice the world around you. London's parks and gardens are still some of the best places to find a moment of peace, whether that's amid the ancient beauty of Queen's Wood (no.19) or wandering through the late-summer lavender in Vauxhall Park (no.39). We've got wild swimming, romantic ruins and nature reserves, all without having to venture further than Zone 2.

When you know where to look, you'll find pockets of peace all over the city – from hushed libraries to still early-morning lidos, pottery classes to horse riding through central London's largest park. Whether you're a seasoned yogi keen to take your practice to the next level or a stressed-out city worker looking to rebalance your life, these are the places to exhale and enjoy a perfect moment of calm.

Christina Rose Brown
London, 2025

Christina is a writer, artist, teacher and mother who lives in a small house in the very centre of London with her kids, husband and dog. It's no wonder she is looking for a bit more calm in her life.

BEST FOR...

Getting back to nature

Whether you're looking for woodland, meadows, rolling hills or wild swimming, sprawling Hampstead Heath (no.18) has it all. To escape the chaos of central London, Phoenix Garden offers a leafy oasis (no.2); and while it might be inside (and right next to Victoria station), there's no better way to feel a connection to the earth than getting your hands dirty at Studio Pottery London (no.54).

Moving your body

Exercise in any form will combat stress, whether it's gentle yoga stretches at beginner-friendly Yoga on the Lane (no.31) or an outdoor dip – made possible (and pleasurable) all year round thanks to London Fields Lido's (no.27) heated pool. For the more adventurous, saddling up and taking a canter round Hyde Park with one of the steeds of Ross Nye Stables (no.51) will get those endorphins flowing.

All the family

East of Eden (no.32) offers yoga classes for toddlers and older children, while a walk through the wild Queen's Wood (no.19) provides opportunities for forest bathing or tree-climbing. The simulated space exploration at the Planetarium (no.45) is so awe-inspiring that even the chattiest kids will be stunned into silence.

Working and thinking

Host Cafe (no.6), an Anglican-church-turned-coffee-spot, offers bookable work spaces with hot drinks and stunning surroundings. The British Library's (no.20) Reading Rooms are quiet, central and completely free to use. And if you're in need of a moment of introspection, Inner Temple Gardens (no.1) offers plenty of places to sit and ponder.

Treating yourself

You won't find anything more luxurious than the sumptuous subterranean spa of the St. Pancras Renaissance Hotel (no.26). Petersham Nurseries Teahouse (no.41) is the home of fresh fine dining, or Inhabit will ensure your best-ever night's sleep (no.61).

Going with a friend

Join an (alcohol-free) cocktail class at Club Soda (no.7) for a great evening out without any of the associated headaches or hangxiety, or catch up over homely vegetarian plates at the community-run Bonnington Cafe (no.37).

A spiritual reset

Whatever your persuasion, we've got you covered. Learn to meditate with a Buddhist monk at Buddhapadipa Temple (no.42), or visit the serene Islamic Gardens of the Aga Khan Centre (no.25). Candlelit Evensong at St Martin-in-the-Fields (no.4) is a thing of transcendental beauty, or if you're more New Age than evangelical, stock up on crystals and tarot cards at Soulstice (no.15).

1

INNER TEMPLE GARDENS

The city's courtyard garden

Not only is this grand three-acre garden slap-bang in the middle of central London, but it gets a shout-out from Shakespeare, with a scene from *Henry VI* taking place on its manicured lawns. There's been a garden on this site since the 1100s, but despite its location and impressive history, it somehow flies under the radar, making it the perfect place to escape the throngs of tourists nearby. Totally enclosed and only open to the public on weekday lunchtimes (12:30–3pm), it feels like a country estate, with gently undulating hills, wildflower borders and stately trees – if it weren't for the ever-present rumble of buses on Victoria Embankment that never quite let you forget where you are.

Temple, EC4Y 7HB
Nearest station: Temple
innertemple.org.uk

2

THE PHOENIX GARDEN

Lush refuge from the West End

Just a hop, skip and jump away from the madness of Covent Garden is this halcyon hideaway, home to a plethora of plants and wildlife – including a family of urban frogs. The sheltered inner-city location creates a unique microclimate, allowing for sub-tropical fauna such as a colossal Giant Viper's Bugloss to thrive alongside wild pear trees and wisteria. Built on the site of an old car park, this is the last remaining of seven original community gardens in the area. The garden is managed with the natural philosophy of no weeds, no pests and no waste, resulting in a flourishing space that is both low maintenance and laid-back – a feeling that spreads to all who recuperate here.

1 Stacey Street, WC2H 8DG
Nearest station: Tottenham Court Road
thephoenixgarden.org

3

ST DUNSTAN-
IN-THE-EAST

London's most peaceful bombsite

No matter what time you arrive at this romantic ruin, you are bound to find at least one photographer setting up a shot. One of London's most picturesque green spaces, this ancient church was bombed during the Second World War and never rebuilt. Now, it's like an otherworldly, abandoned film set, the creeping vines entwined through gothic windows creating an irresistible backdrop for selfie-takers. But don't let that put you off. A stone's throw from the Square Mile, this is an astonishingly peaceful spot for a moment of solitude or secluded lunch. Visit in the spring when the overhanging trees burst into pastel-pink blossom and dappled light dances through the foliage.

St Dunstan's Hill, EC3R 5DD
Nearest station: Monument
cityoflondon.gov.uk

4

ST MARTIN-IN-
THE-FIELDS

Elegant Anglican evensong

You don't need to be religious to appreciate the exquisite beauty of a church, and you don't need to be a classical music connoisseur to feel the emotional impact of a choral crescendo. Inside the gilded grandeur of St Martin-in-the-Fields, amid flickering candles, the swell of the orchestra feels particularly transcendental. Concerts run for an hour every Saturday evening, with a couple of midweek shows per month (tickets start at a tenner). The contemporary stained-glass window by artist Shirazeh Houshiary depicting an abstracted cross, as if reflected in water, is a minimalist masterpiece and offers a focal point for a moment of mindful meditation amid the majestic music.

Trafalgar Square, WC2N 4JJ
Nearest station: Charing Cross
stmartin-in-the-fields.org

5

OLD STREET SPA EXPERIENCE

Affordable subterranean spa

Don't let the location – in the basement of a public swimming pool – fool you. This hidden treasure is every bit as luxurious as some of London's swankiest hotel spas, and doesn't require a king's ransom. The cavernous space houses multiple intriguing rooms. Pick the juniper-infused sauna to gently soothe aching muscles, or a salt steam for a natural serotonin boost, then (if you're feeling brave) cool down with arctic mist. With ambient music and gentle birdsong played throughout, and fluffy robes provided, this slice of paradise feels a million miles away from the Old Street Roundabout.

1 Norman Street, EC1V 3AA
Nearest station: Old Street
Other locations: see website
spaexperience.org.uk

6

HOST CAFE

Heavenly coffee on hallowed ground

Slip into a pew and take in the divine surroundings of this working church and cafe. Having (just about) survived the Great Fire of London and then the Blitz, this Gothic Revival gem – designed by Sir Christopher Wren – can tell you a thing or two about stability. The high plaster ceiling and Victorian stained-glass windows give light and airy ecclesiastical elegance, the smell of coffee mingling with Anglican incense. Lunchtimes can be busy with a flock of city workers, so come early to sit with a herbal tea and enjoy this sacred space at its most peaceful.

St Mary Aldermary, Watling Street, EC4M 9BW
Nearest station: Mansion House
hostcafelondon.com

7

CLUB SODA

Mindful low- and no-alcohol drinks

London's most innovative cocktails are not coming out of a basement speakeasy in Soho, but the bijou tasting room of this booze-free bottle shop. Unwind over Smoky Palomas – made with a no-alcohol amber spirit and infused with chilli – while enjoying all the mental health benefits of an evening socialising without any of the anxiety or disturbed sleep that come with overdoing it. Whether you're totally abstaining, sober-curious or just looking for alternative options, join a cocktail-making masterclass or prop up the bar with a 0% sparkling chardonnay or CBD-infused kombucha. You'll never be stuck nursing a pint of lime and soda again.

39 Drury Lane, WC2B 5RR
Nearest station: Covent Garden
joinclubsoda.com

8

MASAJ

A thoroughly modern massage

There are records that show massage has been practised since 3,000 BCE. MASAJ bring that ancient knowledge up to date with a bijou range of simplified treatment options designed to combat the stress of city life, all delivered to a soundtrack of transcendental soundscapes and velvety contemporary jazz. Spend your days hunched over a computer? Drop in for a deep tissue massage to melt away muscle knots and combat the dreaded 'tech neck'. Overwhelmed by the London grind? Choose a relaxing massage with gentler touch to create a sense of tranquillity and lower your heart rate. Never have time for yourself? Fear not: with appointments up until 9pm, you can fit it in, however precarious your work–life balance.

10 Charlotte Road, EC2A 3DH
Nearest station: Old Street
Other location: Marylebone
masaj.me

TAILOR YOUR MASAJ //

SOUND // Pick a Playlist

☐ **VELVET**
A dreamy hybrid of classical and contemporary jazz and piano selections. Totally non verbal for a soft peaceful pause.

☐ **STILLNESS**
An amalgamation of all our favourite tracks and genres to seamlessly guide you, through your bodywork. From our ears and hearts to yours.

☑ **NECTAR**
A sweet drizzle

SCENT // Choose your M

☐ **EVE**
A slumber inducing aroma with citrus crispness and a subtly woody tone. Take me to stillness.
Lavender, Mandarin and Vetiver blended in Grapeseed and Jojoba

☐ **WATERSHED**
An earthy and tender blend to dulcify busy minds. Delicate, softening.
Cedarwood, Carrot Seed, German Chamomile and Roman Chamomile blended in Sunflower seed and Evening Primrose

☐ **SU**
A ref
away k
spring in t
*Basil, Berga
blended in Gr*

WORDS // Let us know your

QUIET
I'm here to totally zone out

☐
MASAJ C
Relax and f

9

26 GRAINS

Nourish yourself

As the three bears would tell you, there is nothing more comforting than a good bowl of porridge. And those cooked oats won't just fill you up; they can also calm inflammation in the gut and help with serotonin production. This wholesome pocket restaurant tucked away in Neal's Yard is dedicated to all things grain-based, including sourdough toast topped with eggs fried in chilli butter or garlic mushrooms. It's the elevated sweet and savoury porridges made with their signature five-grain mix, though, that steal the show. Like a warm hug in a bowl, it's just right.

1 Neal's Yard, WC2H 9DP
Nearest station: Covent Garden
26grains.com

10

TARA YOGA CENTRE

Free flow yoga for all

You won't be sent straight into a plank in one of these sessions; classes are spiritual and focused on reconnecting the soul, body and breath to achieve total harmony, rather than working up a sweat. In fact, you're more likely to doze off during the meditation than pull a muscle. Best of all, the thrice-weekly evening hatha sessions are completely free, making this a truly accessible studio. Each night has a different wellbeing focus, so whether you're looking to spark joy or gain inner peace, pick what feels right for you.

25–31 Ironmonger Row, EC1V 3QW
Nearest station: Old Street
tarayogacentre.co.uk

11

INNER SPACE

Bookshop and meditation centre

If you had to name the *least* calming activity in London, navigating Oxford Street would probably take the crown. Luckily for frazzled shoppers and city-dwellers, Inner Space – nestled on a slightly more subdued Covent Garden street – is on hand to help us escape the overwhelm. Upstairs is a bookshop selling guides to meditation and personal growth; downstairs, the 'Quiet Room' is available for anyone in need of a moment of peace. All events are free, including the thrice-weekly guided meditations, a concise 20-minute session that fits conveniently into a lunchbreak. Looking to go deeper? Regular hour-long seminars explore weighty topics such as self-belief and practising gratitude.

36 Short's Gardens, WC2H 9AB
Nearest station: Covent Garden
innerspace.org.uk

12

NEAL'S YARD REMEDIES

Veterans of natural wellbeing

Neal's Yard have been bottling organic botanicals for over 40 years. And while you can now pick up their products in supermarkets, the original Covert Garden shop is still a bona fide destination for relaxation. Not sure where to start? The Goodnight Pillow Mist is a classic, with naturally grounding vetiver alongside mandarin essential oil, thought to uplift mood and reduce anxiety, so even the busiest of minds will be set for a night of peaceful sleep. Hop across the yard to their therapy room for an aromatherapy massage using one of their signature oil blends (or some manual lymphatic drainage if you're feeling more adventurous), then next door to 26 Grains (no.9) for a wholesome (and delicious) lunch.

15 Neal's Yard, WC2H 9DP
Nearest station: Covent Garden
nealsyardremedies.com

13

KATSUTE100

Tranquil Japanese tea house

There's nothing like a good cup of tea to soothe the soul, and these guys know a thing or two about good tea. Katsute100's range of rare teas include magnesium-rich Kuromamecha, and Gyokuro, a high-grade green tea shade-grown 21 days before harvest. These are imported directly from artisanal producers in Japan, where tea drinking is an important cultural activity and tea ceremonies are practised to promote harmony with nature and discipline the mind. Choose a cup of Genmaicha, a green tea blended with aromatic roasted rice, for a toasty, comforting brew, and take a seat among the trailing vines in their verdant garden. Drink in that moment of zen.

100 Islington High Street, N1 8EG
Nearest station: Angel
Other locations: Brick Lane, Covent Garden
katsute100.com

14

BLOMMA BEAUTY

Feel-good natural beauty

Sitting in a shop in Angel getting your forehead prodded by a stranger might not sound that relaxing, but the folks here are experts in nourishing your face, body and soul with beauty products that go more than skin-deep. Book in for a restorative facial using all natural, organic ingredients (including wild rosehip oils harvested from the foothills of the Chilean Andes) and you'll be glowing from the inside out. Feeling stressed? Pick up a dose of tranquillity to-go with a geranium and frankincense roll-on remedy to soothe overstimulated senses.

Omnia Holistic Centre, 16b Essex Road,
Off Colebrooke Row, N1 8LN
Nearest station: Angel
blommabeauty.com

15

SOULSTICE

New Age healing for the well-heeled

This Insta-worthy crystal shop is a far cry from the dusty spell books and clouds of patchouli incense that you may remember from the witchy shops of your teenage years. Here, the amethysts come set in chic rose gold jewellery and rose quartz crystals top luxury scented candles. New to the world of woo woo? Peruse the trays of pastel-hued gemstones and pick one based on the outcome promised, from uplift to mental clarity. Ready to take the next step? Drift away in their nearby Soul Studio to the tones of a crystal singing bowl during one of their immersive sound baths – no undressing required, just lie down and meditate on the resonant chimes, proven to reduce stress and prompt relaxation.

107 Regents Park Road, NW1 8UR
Nearest station: Chalk Farm
soulsticelondon.com

16

WELLCOME READING ROOM

Chilled museum library

The Wellcome's Reading Room is home to all manner of fascinating artworks, objects and books related to health and the human condition, from an imposing-looking antique dentist's light to ancient fertility statues. With plenty of comfy sofas and hidden reading nooks, it maintains the peace of a library but without any of the stuffiness. Activities are dotted around, inviting the curious to engage with the collection – there's even a mirrored self-portrait station if you're feeling creative. For a truly relaxing visit, skip the shelf labelled 'Pain, Childbirth, Anesthesia' and curl up with a book on mindfulness on one of the squishy, oversized cushions that line the central staircase.

183 Euston Road, NW1 2BE
Nearest station: Euston Square
wellcomecollection.org

17

CAMDEN ART CENTRE

Restorative gallery and gardens

Keen to harness the positive mental health benefits of creativity but overwhelmed by the thought
of picking up a paintbrush? Fear not: just looking at art is proven to reduce stress, release
feel-good endorphins and combat feelings of lone-
liness. Dodge the crowds that flock to London's
most famous art institutions with this light-filled
gallery in leafy Hampstead. Peruse exhibitions
from boundary-pushing contemporary artists,
then retire to the serene garden to discover more
hidden artworks – such as Aaron McPeake's *Toll*,
a bell suspended from an ash tree, which visitors
are invited to ring. Or just sit back with a glass
of something cold from the cafe and meditate on
what you've seen.

Arkwright Road, NW3 6DG
Nearest station: Finchley Road & Frognal
camdenartcentre.org

18

HAMPSTEAD HEATH

The capital's countryside escape

London's rural idyll, the Heath offers all the benefits of country life without the stress of leaving the city. For a boost of endorphins, a dip in one of the three swimming ponds (one for men, one for women and one mixed) is unbeatable. The facilities may be a little rustic and the water a murky shade of green, but there's an undeniable charm to swimming here. Herons swoop overhead and iridescent dragonflies dance around the banks. Set aside a whole day for a restorative ramble over the Heath's rolling hills, meadows and ancient woodlands, and don't forget to refuel with a satisfying slab of cake in the Kenwood House cafe.

Nearest Station: Hampstead Heath
hampsteadheath.net

19

QUEEN'S WOOD

Historic woodland for forest bathing

The Japanese have known for generations about the benefits of spending time in the woods, calling this *shinrin-yoku* (literally, forest bathing). Contrary to what the literal translation might suggest, this practice isn't about water; rather, forest bathing involves paying careful attention to your woodland surroundings to ground yourself in the moment. There is nowhere better in London to do so than the majestic Queen's Wood in Highgate. Take off your headphones and fully immerse yourself: hear the fallen leaves crunch underfoot, see the dappled light peeking through the canopy and smell the earthy aroma of the oak trees. Come in the spring to see the bluebells, and look (or listen) for one of the three native species of woodpecker who call this wood home.

Queen's Wood Road, N6 6UU
Nearest station: Highgate

20

THE BRITISH LIBRARY

Serene study space

Is there anything more comforting than the smell of old books? And it's not just down to nostalgia: as organic compounds in the pages of ageing tomes break down, they give off a musky vanilla scent – like an olfactory hug. Where better to get a whiff of all the old books your heart desires than the British Library, home to every book ever published in the UK, plus a bevy of rare historical manuscripts? Most are stored away in underground vaults, but sign up for a (free) Reader's Pass and you'll be granted access to the hushed Reading Rooms (which make excellent study spots) and have the ability to request from the 170 million+ catalogue.

96 Euston Road, NW1 2DB
Nearest station: King's Cross
bl.uk

21

DOWN TO EARTH

Sun salutations with style

One of the most well-established independent yoga studios in London, Down to Earth has been serving the debonair yogis of Tufnell Park for over ten years. Founder Vanda is a St Martins graduate, and her artistic touch has transformed every inch of this space, from the abstract mural in muted shades of blush and slate, to the plants in mismatched ceramic pots. Housed in an elegant former piano factory, the snug treatment rooms and two light-drenched pilates and yoga studios (draped with twinkling fairy lights for evening Yin classes) open onto a private cobbled courtyard – a secluded spot in which to pause after class if you're not quite ready to face the world again.

225 & 225a, Brecknock Road, N19 5AA
Nearest station: Tufnell Park
downtoearthlondon.co.uk

22

SACRED HARMONY REIKI

Modern mystical healing

Nestled among the Turkish restaurants and convenience stores of Stoke Newington High Street is a secret and sacred reiki studio. Founder Ricky is part of the next generation of New Age, combining his experience in ancient Japanese energy healing with modern coaching techniques and a cool mid-century style (the studio is decked out in walnut furniture and leafy monsteras). Book in for a 'Rejuvenation Reiki' session, a hands-on treatment where gentle, non-invasive touch is used to channel energy throughout the body to bring about a profound sense of relaxation.

81 Stoke Newington Road, N16 8AD
Nearest station: Dalston Kingsland
sacredharmonyreiki.co.uk

23

BALIGA CLINIC

Holistic healthcare from ancient India

Ayurveda – a 3,000-year-old holistic health system that uses natural approaches like diet, breathwork and yoga to keep the mind, body and spirit healthy – is considered as important as modern medicine in India. Practitioners like Dr Raghav Baliga train for over five years, studying everything from human anatomy to ancient Sanskrit. In his Hoxton clinic, treatments are adjusted to your balance of *doshas* (life forces) through personalised herb oils and massage strokes. For maximum relaxation, opt for Shirodhara, where body-temperature oil is slowly dripped onto the centre of the forehead – an ancient practice that has been shown to reduce stress.

66 Nile Street, N1 7SR
Nearest station: Old Street
baliga.clinic

24

CONSERVATORY ARCHIVES

The secret garden (centre)

Hidden down an unassuming path off a residential road in north London, this former Victorian stable is home to an ever-growing menagerie of horticultural delights. Outside, the artfully dishevelled display feels more like a cool urban backyard than a traditional nursery; inside, it's crammed to the (antique) rafters with giant palms, trailing philodendrons and snappy succulents. Just browsing amid the foliage here is an immensely peaceful experience, but with house plants touted as the secret to stress reduction, it's well worth taking a few home.

3 Middleton Mews, N7 9LT
Nearest station: Caledonian Road
Other location: Lower Clapton
conservatoryarchives.co.uk

25

ISLAMIC GARDENS, AGA KHAN CENTRE

Paradise above King's Cross

That the word paradise comes from the Persian for garden should tell you everything you need to know about how seriously landscaping is taken in the Islamic world. The Aga Khan Centre, a temple to learning with a focus on Islamic studies, is home to six idyllic outdoor spaces inspired by the diversity of Muslim culture. The largest, The Garden of Life, includes four areas divided by flowing water, with fruit trees and jasmine to symbolise abundance. These tranquil terraces are usually the reserve of Aga Khan University staff and students, but lay-people can gain entry via twice-weekly volunteer-run tours, which are free (but book up quickly).

10 Handyside Street, N1C 4DN
Nearest station: King's Cross
agakhancentre.org.uk

26

ST. PANCRAS SPA

Victorian splendour, contemporary wellness

In keeping with the gothic elegance of one of London's most iconic hotels, the spa at the St. Pancras Renaissance – accessible with a day pass if you're not staying over – is inspired by grand Victorian bathhouses. This opulent underground sanctuary incorporates elements of traditional hammams, such as Moroccan tiles and mood lighting, with the original features of the building (the high arches once housed stoves and fire pits when this space was the kitchen). Everything here is designed to make you feel incredibly well looked after, from the comfy poolside loungers to the cloudlike fluffy robes. The sapphire-blue hydrotherapy pool is so warm that it feels like stepping into a bath, and treatment beds come with blankets and pillows.

Euston Road, NW1 2AR
Nearest station: Euston
stpancras-spa.com

27
LONDON FIELDS LIDO

East London's favourite pool

This Hackney institution certainly pulls in a throng of dedicated locals on sunny days – and understandably so, with its 50-metre Olympic-sized pool and paved areas perfect for soaking up some rays. But if the thought of swimming through the crowds is off-putting, come on a cooler day when the lanes are far emptier. Besides the azure water and rainbow-hued bunting strung above, the beauty of London Fields Lido is that it's heated, so you can enjoy the stress-busting benefits of an alfresco dip year-round. Though if you *do* need to warm up or refuel post-swim, then a hot chocolate and locally baked croissant from the adjoining pool-side cafe will be just the ticket.

London Fields West Side, E8 3EU
Nearest station: London Fields
better.org.uk

28

BODIED

Massage studio open to all

A stack of shipping containers off Hackney Road might seem an unlikely wellness destination, but inside these corrugated iron walls is a boutique studio with a difference. Founded in 2021 with an aim of making massage treatments more accessible to global majority communities, Bodied specialise in personalised deep tissue and sports massage. They pay careful attention to creating a calm, comfortable and empowered space, collaborating with local charities to raise awareness of the benefits of bodywork. You can even select the scent of the oils used and specify how chatty you'd like your therapist to be via your pre-treatment questionnaire.

19–20 Gossamer Gardens, E2 9FN
Nearest station: Cambridge Heath
bodied.co.uk

29

COMMUNITY SAUNA BATHS

Reviving sauna complex

This authentic Finnish wood-fired sauna is found in the car park of an old bathhouse. Work your way around six communal saunas heated to different temperatures and then cool off with an invigorating (and endorphin-releasing) dunk into a barrel (or bathtub) of freezing water. Be warned: during winter, the cold plunges are an icy 5–8° Celsius (and only a marginally more bearable 10–14° in summer). The busy events calendar also offers plenty more ways to relax, from aromatherapy sessions to queer poetry nights.

80 Eastway, E9 5JH
Nearest station: Hackney Wick
Other locations: Peckham, Bermondsey, Stratford
community-sauna.co.uk

30

UCHI

Homely Japanese fare

It's hard to beat the feeling of getting home and kicking off your shoes. But imagine then being handed a bowl of warm miso soup, chewy balls of deep-fried rice and smoky aubergine cooked over coals until molten. *And* you don't even have to do the washing up. At UCHI, not only does the upstairs room have a no-shoes policy, but they'll lend you a pair of cosy slippers, too (specify you'd like to be upstairs when booking, or risk being confined to your old clodhoppers for the duration of your meal). Along with the elevated home-cooked dishes and perfectly mismatched crockery, it will come as no surprise to regulars that *uchi* means home in Japanese.

144 Clarence Road, E5 8DY
Nearest station: Clapton
uchihackney.com

31

YOGA ON THE LANE

London's friendliest yoga studio

This could so easily be just another oh-so-trendy east London studio, but from the moment you are handed a cup of pre-class herbal tea, you'll realise Yoga on the Lane is an especially welcoming experience. The focus here is not on designer gym outfits or competitive headstands; rather, it's about creating an inclusive space for all yogis. Whether it's the palpably cosy vibe (with underfloor heating to keep you toasty during your savasana), the parent-and-baby sessions offering restorative support to postpartum mothers or the regular super clubs – which combine gentle movement and sound meditations with a chance to natter over bowls of home-cooked dahl – you'll leave feeling thoroughly nourished.

105 Shacklewell Lane, E8 2EB
Nearest station: Dalston Kingsland
yogaonthelane.com

32

EAST OF EDEN

Easygoing exercise classes

Founded as a small neighbourhood studio, East of Eden now hosts over 100 classes a week in everything from outdoor meditation (in collaboration with the local council) to sensory-adapted spin classes, ideal for anyone who would benefit from softer lighting and calmer vibes. The Sunday evening Yin yoga might be the best way to end the week. Poses are held for several minutes, allowing for deeper stretches and giving space for the parasympathetic nervous system to slow. And because no one needs calming down more than a three-year-old, they also offer monthly yoga sessions for toddlers and drop-off classes for older kids (while you enjoy some peace with a turmeric latte in the cafe downstairs). Namaste.

14 Hatherley Mews, E17 4QP
Nearest station: Walthamstow
eastofeden.uk

33

BETHNAL GREEN NATURE RESERVE

East End gone wild

This picturesque woodland garden has been cultivated and cared for by volunteers since 1977. Located on a former WWII bombsite, it's now a sanctuary for the myriad species who call it home (look out for the towering abstract wooden sculpture, a collaboration between artist DJ Simpson and ecologist Olly Edmonds specially designed to house a population of Pipistrelle bats inside its cosy chambers). As well as the gloriously overgrown woods, there's a mushroom farm, pond and medicinal meadow. Visit the reserve on Saturday afternoons from May to November, or join a volunteer gardening morning or natural dye workshop.

Middleton Street, E2 9RR
Nearest station: Bethnal Green
bethnalgreennaturereserve.org

34

THE WELL GARDEN

Tranquil treatments for stressed urbanites

Upon entering this holistic healing centre, housed among the creative community of Hackney Downs Studios, you'll be swathed in the scent of warm, woody frankincense. Here, co-owners Samantha and Darren and their team of practitioners offer everything from herbal medicine consultations to combat emotional imbalances, to reflexology (which releases stored tension throughout the entire body by applying pressure to the soles of the feet). Even experts disagree on exactly how this works (some say the massage unblocks static energy, others think points in the feet are connected to our nervous system), but one thing's for sure: after an hour-long foot-rub or bespoke aromatherapy consultation, you'll be walking on air.

17 Amhurst Terrace, E8 2BT
Nearest station: Rectory Road
thewellgarden.co.uk

35

SHE'S LOST CONTROL

Calming crystal shop

Step off busy Broadway Market into She's Lost Control, and you will instantly feel the energy shift. The shop has been carefully designed to ease the nervous system, from the feng shui-informed layout to the nude cement walls infused with selenite dust. There are even collections of crystals hidden under the floor to maintain the positive energy flow. Embrace your modern witch as you browse handmade incense sticks and fine crystal jewellery (made in their on-site workshop), or book in for a tarot reading or aura photography. And to top it all off, SLC are leading the charge in ethical crystals, so you can be sure that any bought here have been mined sustainably.

74 Broadway Market, E8 4QJ
Nearest station: London Fields
sheslostcontrol.co.uk

36

ROOT/25

Great coffee and even better ethics

Breathing life into a former funeral parlour, the family team behind human rights organisation Restless Beings created this cosy community cafe to support the charity's vital work. Relax on comfy leather sofas or settle down with your laptop among the bookshelves in their library area (nearly every table has a plug) and tuck into homemade Indian-spiced jaggery and chai cake. Poetry nights, 'Sip and Paint' evenings and supper clubs bring the local community together and raise vital aid for Palestine, and there's even a quiet prayer space downstairs for anyone who needs it.

116b Bow Road, E3 3AA
Nearest station: Bow Road
restlessbeings.org

37

BONNINGTON CAFE

Community-focused comfort food

This living room-turned-vegetarian-cafe has been serving up hearty, home-cooked fare from a roster of chefs for over 40 years. A few minutes' away from the mayhem of Vauxhall station, the cafe was founded as part of a resident-led renovation of Bonnington Square, which saw squatters occupying bomb-damaged houses and creating a tropical community garden. The menu changes daily, serving up everything from traditional Syrian recipes passed down from grandparents to American comfort classics, all at affordable prices. Take a seat by the fireplace, surrounded by locals and families, and savour food that's been made with love. If that doesn't get you feeling all warm and fuzzy, I don't know what will.

11 Vauxhall Grove, sw8 1td
Nearest station: Vauxhall
bonningtoncentre.org

38

LEVITATE

Everyday enlightenment

Not all heroes wear capes – and not all mindfulness gurus wear robes. Levitate founder Ryan is more likely to be sporting a plaid shirt and jeans than a yellow kasya when he opens the door of his Victorian townhouse and invites you into his cosy home–studio. And it's not just his attire that brings meditation down to earth. A self-confessed former sceptic, Ryan steers away from anything too woo woo, backing up his experience of the healing power of meditation with neuroscientific research. His weekly Monday night class features a 45-minute meditation (though many previous 'levitators' say it feels more like ten), followed by half an hour of conversation with fellow attendees over a cup of herbal tea.

Sprules Road, SE4 2NL
Nearest station: Brockley
levitate.london

39

VAUXHALL PARK LAVENDER GARDEN

London's only lavender field

Ok, so calling it a field is a bit of a stretch. This patch of Fawcett Gardens within Vauxhall Park might lack the scale and drama of a Provence lavender farm, but it makes up for this with its convenient location. That sweet floral scent is so much more than an ingredient for bubble baths: lavender contains linalool, a compound believed to slow the nervous system and reduce anxiety. Visit between May and late August to see the flowers in full bloom before their early September harvest, and look out for the limited bottles of oil pressed from the park's plants in local shops and markets come December.

Vauxhall Park, SW8 1JY
Nearest station: Vauxhall
vauxhallpark.org.uk

40

BECKENHAM PLACE PARK SWIMMING LAKE

Expansive setting for a cold dip

If you've ever met an open water swimming enthusiast, you'll be all too aware of just *how beneficial* they find their outdoor dips. Admittedly, these evangelical claims *do* seem to be backed up by science, with cold water said to boost dopamine and serotonin levels. Even if it is technically artificial, this South London lake is one of the best places in London for a wild swim (along with the Hampstead ponds, no.18). Lined by majestic alder trees and populated by fish, ducks and bugs aplenty, it's open year-round – but the water feels chilly even at the height of summer, so pack a warm jumper and a flask of tea.

Beckenham Hill Road, BR3 1SY
Nearest station: Beckenham Hill
beckenhamplacepark.com

41

PETERSHAM NURSERIES TEAHOUSE

Verdant dining

There is nothing like the feel of the earth underfoot to make you feel grounded. And there probably aren't many other Michelin-starred restaurants with a bare dirt floor. It just shows that the team here are committed to fostering a connection with nature – whether you're crunching on just-picked veggies from the kitchen garden (battered in tempura and served in delectable stacks) or gathering plant cuttings to nurture at home. Mismatched vintage furniture, strung lights and abundant, artfully unkempt foliage give a relaxed vibe that belies the absolute excellence of it all.

Off Church Lane, Petersham Road, TW10 7AB
Nearest station: Richmond
petershamnurseries.com

42

BUDDHAPADIPA TEMPLE

Welcoming sacred space

Looking to reach Nirvana? Enlightenment might be waiting for you at the end of the District line. This ornate Buddhist temple next to Wimbledon Common looks like it's been transported straight from the mountains of Khao Chi Chan. It's fully consecrated (as the monks wrapped in orange robes will attest to) and under the patronage of the Thai Royal Family, but is free to enter and open to all. Surrealist murals by Thai artists line the walls and gold statues abound. The gardens are also worth exploring, with oriental bridges that cross trickling streams and prayer flags strung between trees. Visit at the weekend (3–5pm) to learn meditation techniques from the masters of mindfulness.

14 Calonne Road, SW19 5HJ
Nearest station: Wimbledon
watbuddhapadipa.org

43

NATIONAL POETRY LIBRARY

Repository for rhymes and verse

Ready to immerse yourself in the healing potential of the written word? Head for the home of modern and contemporary poetry in the UK, tucked away on level 5 of the Royal Festival Hall and cast in a warm, welcoming glow thanks to the yellow-tinted glass door. The library is open to all, though if you want to borrow books you'll need to join as a member (for free, just bring ID). Explicitly not a general study space, it is reserved for those who wish to browse the collection or work on their own verse, with plenty of nooks in which to sit and read.

Southbank Centre, SE1 8XX
Nearest station: Waterloo
southbankcentre.co.uk

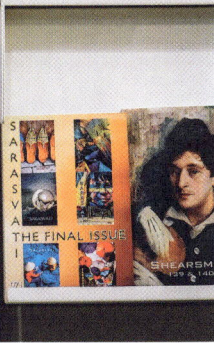

T
E
I
T
O
R
N
Y
Reference Author
← TR – WH WH – Z →
Magazine
A – B
Reference
Anthologies
A – AN →
Reference
Anthologies
← AN – EX
Reference
Anthologies
← LY – PA PA – SE →
SE – Z
C
O

A

L

L

I

B

Magazines
← E   E–I   →

Magazines
← I–M   M–P   →

Magazines
← P   P–S   →

Magazines
← S–V   W–Z
      Zines   →

Loan Authors
A – AM   →

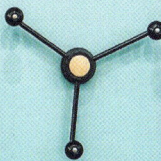

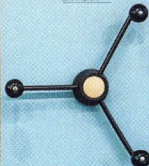

L

L

E

C

44

ROTHKO ROOM, TATE MODERN

Meditative murals from a modern master

When these paintings were first gifted to the Tate, they came with precise instructions from the artist on how they should be displayed, including the exact height from the floor, the pale grey shade for the walls and, most importantly, the (lack of) lighting. These wishes have been honoured, and the unlit room is a distinct contrast to the bright spotlights and stark white typically associated with galleries. Rothko's grand works, in sombre shades of maroon and deep red, have a transcendental beauty and hypnotic pull; time stands still in their presence. Both the work and the setting come together to create a uniquely contemplative space that showcases the emotional power of art.

Bankside, SE1 9TG
Nearest station: Blackfriars
tate.org.uk

45

PLANETARIUM, ROYAL OBSERVATORY GREENWICH

Interstellar inspiration

Contemplating the vastness of the cosmos and our tiny place within it could either bring on a profound feeling of peace, or spark an existential crisis. Thankfully, scientific evidence suggests that the former is much more likely. Stargazing in London can be tricky given all the pesky light pollution, but under the dome of the Planetarium everything shines brightly. Daily shows explore the sky as it will be that evening, with immersive projections, while Morning Stars sessions offer a quieter, sensory-adapted display for autistic individuals. Lean back on the plush velvet recliner, and look up to ponder the meaning of life, the universe and everything.

Blackheath Avenue, SE10 8XJ
Nearest station: Maze Hill
rmg.co.uk/royal-observatory

46

FLOATWORKS

Sensory deprivation for maximum relaxation

The thought of imprisoning yourself in a plastic space-pod filled with water might sound totally terror-inducing, but an hour in one of the tanks at Floatworks supposedly *lowers* levels of anxiety. Put aside any thoughts of entrapment and allow yourself to be held by the buoyant water, heated to body temperature and thick with Epsom salt to create a seemingly weightless sensation. Surrounded by darkness and cut off from the cacophony of the city, your brain can enter into a meditative state of deep relaxation. All the while your body is absorbing magnesium from the salt, which helps balance stress hormones and soothe aching muscles.

17b St George Wharf, sw8 2LE
Nearest station: Vauxhall
Other location: Angel
floatworks.com

47

FINNISH CHURCH SAUNA

Scandi-style basement hot-box

An old Finnish proverb states that there are two places one can consider holy: the church and the sauna. Kill two birds with one (steaming hot sauna) stone with a visit to this subterranean sweat-lodge. Don't expect luxury – there are no fluffy towels or free slippers here – but it might just be the most authentic sauna experience this side of Helsinki (traditionalists go naked, but swimwear is accepted). Regular heat therapy has been shown to improve mental health; it's no wonder Finland, where the sauna is a cultural touchstone, con-sistently tops the world happiness polls. In their homeland, saunas are considered a social space too, so expect lively conversations between the regulars. *Pitää hauskaa!* (Have fun!)

33 Albion Street, SE16 7HZ
Nearest station: Rotherhithe
britannia.merimieskirkko.fi

48

SHAMBHALA MEDITATION CENTRE

Traditional Buddhist teachings

This Buddhist centre off Clapham High street isn't as glossy as some of the newer meditation studios in the book, and the 'welcome time' spent sat in a circle of chairs feels a little like a village meeting, but the knowledge and expertise here is unparalleled. Built on Buddhist principles of loving kindness, Shambhala is a truly inclusive meditation centre hosting free weekly sessions that are open all, regardless of faith or experience. Newbies will be directed upstairs for an induction on techniques and philosophies before rejoining the main group, while traditional walking meditations provide a challenge to anyone who feels they've mastered it sitting still.

27 Belmont Close, SW4 6AY
Nearest station: Clapham Common
shambhala.org.uk

49

ISABELLA PLANTATION

Elegant wooded sanctuary

Hidden within the wilds of Richmond Park is a secret garden. Filled with swathes of bluebells and babbling streams, under a canopy of beech, oak and sweet chestnut, this is a masterpiece of Victorian woodland planning. The 40-acre site was enclosed in 1830, with fences designed to keep the park's resident deer out (allowing for a greater diversity of fauna). It's always worth seeing the masses of evergreen Azaleas burst into a riot of fuchsia from late April to early May, but the plantation is possibly the best place in London to chart the changing of the seasons – from winter frost to the first sunshine-yellow daffodils of spring.

Richmond Park, TW10 5HS
Nearest station: Richmond
royalparks.org.uk

50

KYOTO GARDEN

The ultimate zen garden

The sound of running water is thought to activate alpha brainwaves, associated with restful and meditative states. London's Kyoto Garden has a trickling stream, a cascading waterfall and an ornamental carp pond. And if that's not enough to get you into a state of deep relaxation, then maybe sitting underneath a maple tree and contemplating the beauty of the surrounding nature will. This tranquil spot was gifted to the UK by Japan in 1991 to commemorate ongoing good relations between the two countries. Visit between late March and April to see the famous Japanese cherry tree crowned in spectacular bright-pink blossom. And if you are truly blessed, you might spot one of the roaming peacocks.

Holland Park, w8 6lu
Nearest station: Holland Park
rbkc.gov.uk

51

ROSS NYE STABLES

The healing power of horses

Queensland-born Ross Nye emigrated to London in the '60s and, missing rural life and the connection to his beloved horses, established a stables in a cobbled mews by Hyde Park to bring riding to central London. Studies show horse riding can stimulate positive psychological feelings and reduce depression – as can anyone attest who's taken one of the Nye steeds out for a hack. Life seems to slow down as you trot through London's premier park, moving in time with the rhythmic pad of hooves and feeling the gentle breeze against your face. This is mindfulness at its most majestic.

8 Bathurst Mews, W2 2SB
Nearest station: Lancaster Gate
rossnyestables.co.uk

52

KLORIS

Premium CBD emporium

Anxiety levels higher than the London skyline? Take a chill pill – but make it a sweet, citrus-flavoured CBD gummy and reap the benefits of this ancient plant medicine. CBD is derived from the cannabis plant and has the same ability to promote relaxation but without any of the psychoactive effects of its illegal cousin. KLORIS's CBD goods are science-backed, ethically sourced and made using all-natural ingredients. The range is built around four pillars of wellness, with products to relieve pain, promote calm, improve sleep or offer menopause support, plus skincare and home spa treatments. Start by trying one of their CBD sleep patches which, unlike sleeping pills, won't cause you to wake up feeling groggy.

13 Newburgh Street, W1F 7RS
Nearest station: Oxford Circus
kloris.co

53

SELF SPACE

Mental health maintenance

Forget everything you think you know about therapy; Self Space is dragging the therapist's couch into the 21st century. There are no waiting lists or drawn-out assessment processes here. Appointments are on-demand, meaning you're not tied to the same slot every week, nor to a particular therapist. Whether you're working through something big, or just want to check in every so often to ensure your mind is as well looked after as your body, you'll be able to find the best person to speak to with their quick online therapist matching service. And if you don't know where to start, a 90-minute Mental Health MOT is a guided appointment that combines gentle therapy with practical life coaching.

95 Berwick Street, W1F 0QB
Nearest station: Piccadilly Circus
Other locations: King's Cross, Shoreditch, Borough
theselfspace.com

SELF SPACE
EVERYDAY MENTAL MAINTENANCE
orary mental
ring a good
a qualified person.
Don't be a stranger
@theselfspace
theselfspace.com
hey@theselfspace.com
020 3935 8788

54

STUDIO POTTERY LONDON

Dirty hands, clear mind

There is nothing more grounding than getting your hands stuck into literal earth. Throwing on the wheel requires your full attention, leaving no space for other thoughts and worries (at least, the ones that aren't about centring your pot). Located in Belgravia's wellness hub (Re:Mind studio, no.56, is just next door) the focus here is on traditional crafts as a counterbalance to fast-paced and increasingly digital modern life. Not sure where to start? Book in for a private lesson to learn and grow in confidence on the wheel. Already a master potter? Sign up for a studio membership to be part of this inspirational creative community. Time to get your hands dirty.

29 Eccleston Place, SW1W 9NF
Nearest station: Victoria
studio-pottery-london.com

55

EARL OF EAST

Comforting lifestyle store

Our olfactory systems are directly linked to memory centres in the brain, meaning a whiff of something familiar can instantly transport us down memory lane. The house fragrance blends at Earl of East are all inspired by the founders' treasured memories of childhood and travel – be it a candle smelling of fresh tomato and herbs from a long Grecian summer, or incense cones that recall English country gardens with sweet jasmine and gardenia. Pick up one of their signature Shinrin-Yoku candles, inspired by Japanese forest bathing rituals, to bring a bit of zen to your home – or join a candle-making workshop to create your own.

Quadrant Arcade, Regent Street, W1B 5RL
Nearest station: Piccadilly Circus
Other locations: Shoreditch, King's Cross, Spitalfields
earlofeast.com

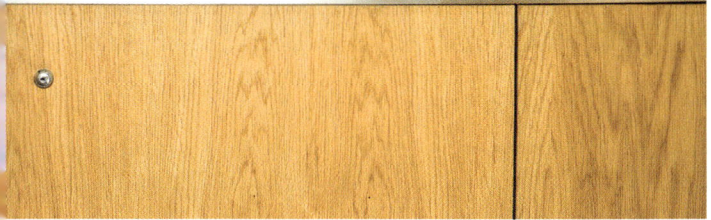

56

RE:MIND

A workout for emotional wellness

If we all took our mental health as seriously as we do our physical, there would be a branch of Re:Mind on every high street. To strengthen your emotional stability, swap out that spin class for some restorative breathwork or somatic movement (where muscles are clenched then released again to decrease tension in the body). Based around three healing pillars of sound, energy and breath, class options here include angelic reiki, crystal bowl meditations and yoga nidra (a deep conscious awareness known as yogic sleep). Afterwards, you can peruse spiritual books and test out oracle cards in their cosy relaxation area with a custom blend of herbal tea. Bliss.

25a Eccleston Place, SW1W 9NF
Nearest station: Victoria
remindstudio.com

57

7 BALI SPA

Tropical treatment rooms

While a retreat in Bali might sound like the ultimate wellness destination, the thought (and cost)
of a 17-hour flight is enough to put off even the
most dedicated yogi. But fear not – you can reap
the benefits of a Balinese massage without ever
leaving central London. 7 Bali's signature 77
Minutes of Inspiration treatment brings a Bali
approach to a traditional Thai massage by using
aromatherapy oil (choose lotus or lavender for
maximum tranquillity). You'll leave feeling like
you've escaped to paradise – even if you're actu-
ally just on your lunch break. Take a moment to
enjoy some complimentary dried fruit and green
tea before stepping back into reality.

11–12 Newman Street, W1T 1PB
Nearest station: Tottenham Court Road
7balispa.co.uk

58

7BREATHS

Ancient wisdom for modern minds

The average person inhales and exhales approximately 22,000 times a day, so you'd think we'd all be experts. But if you've ever felt tense and then realised that you're holding your breath, you'll know it's not quite that simple. Thankfully, 7Breaths are here to help, bringing traditional breathwork and meditation practices from around the world to their luxe central London studio (all mocha tones, natural wood and artfully draped fabric). Join the signature 30-minute class for a taste of deep relaxation which combines guided meditation, controlled breathing and gentle movement, or choose a day retreat for a total nervous system reset. *Ahhhh.*

4 Rathbone Square, W1T 1EB
Nearest station: Tottenham Court Road
7breathsmeditation.com

59

NATIONAL ART LIBRARY, V&A

Blissful archive of art

The hushed atmosphere of the National Art Library is a welcome relief from the often-frantic Victoria and Albert Museum. Inside, the only sound is the muffled chatter of school groups in the surrounding corridors. The walls are lined with row upon row of leatherbound manuscripts documenting the artistic and architectural wonders of the world, alongside exhibition catalogues and the latest copies of trailblazing contemporary art journals. Library members and staff are, understandably, protective of this silent sanctuary; you'll need to register for a reader's ticket (bring ID), leave bags and pens at the door and stay mindfully clear of the rare books.

Cromwell Road, SW7 2RL
Nearest station: South Kensington
vam.ac.uk

60

DAUNT BOOKS

A bookshop to lose yourself in

Feeling the need to get away from it all but lacking the time, money or energy to traipse to Heathrow? Escape to London's most beautiful bookshop instead. Previously home to an antiquarian book-sellers, this building is thought to be the world's first purpose-built bookshop and a destination in its own right, lined with oak shelves, dotted with reading alcoves and bathed in natural light from the original Edwardian conservatory ceiling. Books are divided by country, with travel, food, reference and fiction combined for each region. Browse and be transported from the backstreets of Napoli to the beaches of Bali – all without leaving Marylebone High Street

83 Marylebone High Street, w1u 4qw
Nearest station: Baker Street
Other locations: see website
dauntbooks.co.uk

61

INHABIT

Sublime sleep

It's pretty much the raison d'être of any hotel to create an environment conducive to a good night's sleep, but Inhabit goes the extra mile to make sure its inhabitants leave feeling more rested and renewed than when they arrived. Styled in sleepy shades of sage green and soft blue, rooms are stocked with aromatherapy diffusers, relaxing bedtime reads and vegan pine-infused toiletries. While an overnight stay offers maximum relaxation, anyone can join a yoga class in the tranquil studio, chill in the spa or realign your circadian rhythms with a Serenity Sleep Therapy session.

1–2 Queen's Gardens, W2 3BA
Nearest station: Paddington
Other location: Southwick Street
inhabithotels.com

Selected opinionated guides in the series:

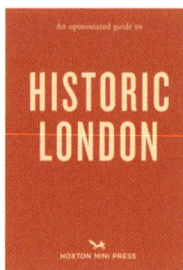

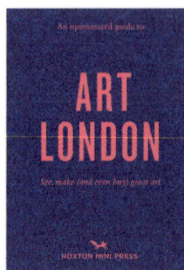

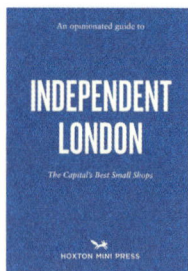

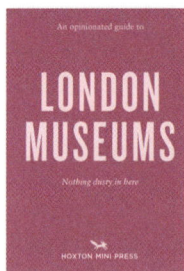

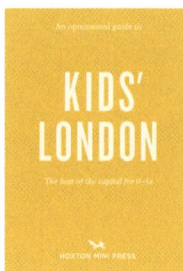

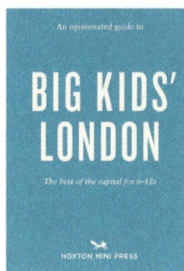

An opinionated guide to
LONDON GREEN SPACES
HOXTON MINI PRESS

An opinionated guide to
HISTORIC LONDON
HOXTON MINI PRESS

An opinionated guide to
ART LONDON
See, make (and even buy) great art
HOXTON MINI PRESS

An opinionated guide to
INDEPENDENT LONDON
The Capital's Best Small Shops
HOXTON MINI PRESS

An opinionated guide to
LONDON BOOKSHOPS
HOXTON MINI PRESS

An opinionated guide to
LONDON MUSEUMS
Nothing dusty in here
HOXTON MINI PRESS

An opinionated guide
ESCAPE LONDON
Day trips and weekends out of the city
HOXTON MINI PRESS

An opinionated guide to
KIDS' LONDON
The best of the capital for 0-11s
HOXTON MINI PRESS

An opinionated guide to
BIG KIDS' LONDON
The best of the capital for 8-12s
HOXTON MINI PRESS

For more go to www.hoxtonminipress.com

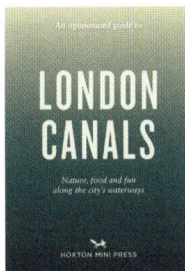

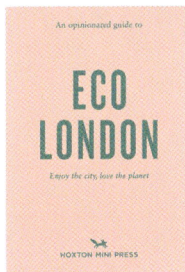

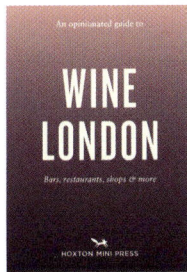

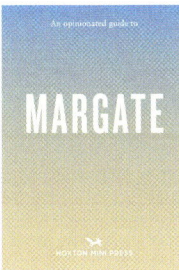

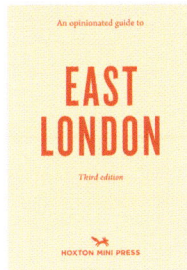

An opinionated guide to

LONDON CANALS

*Nature, food and fun
along the city's waterways*

HOXTON MINI PRESS

An opinionated guide to

FREE LONDON

Enjoy the capital without the cash

HOXTON MINI PRESS

An opinionated guide to

CYCLE LONDON

HOXTON MINI PRESS

An opinionated guide to

ECO LONDON

Enjoy the city, love the planet

HOXTON MINI PRESS

An opinionated guide to

LONDON FOOD

The places you have to try

HOXTON MINI PRESS

An opinionated guide to

WINE LONDON

Bars, restaurants, shops & more

HOXTON MINI PRESS

An opinionated guide to

SOUTH LONDON

HOXTON MINI PRESS

An opinionated guide to

MARGATE

HOXTON MINI PRESS

An opinionated guide to

EAST LONDON

Third edition

HOXTON MINI PRESS

IMAGE CREDITS

An Opinionated Guide to Calm London
First edition

Published in 2025 by Hoxton Mini Press, London
Copyright © Hoxton Mini Press 2025. All rights reserved.

Text by Christina Rose Brown
Editing by Florence Ward
Production design by Dom Grant
Proofreading by Zoë Jellicoe

With thanks to Matthew Young for initial series design.

Please note: we recommend checking the websites listed for each
entry before you visit for the latest information on price, opening times
and pre-booking requirements.

A CIP catalogue record for this book is available from the British Library.

ISBN: 978-1-914314-81-0

Printed and bound by OZGraf, Poland

Hoxton Mini Press is an environmentally conscious publisher, committed
to offsetting our carbon footprint. This book is 100 per cent carbon compensated,
with offset purchased from Stand For Trees.

Every time you order from our website, we plant a tree:
www.hoxtonminipress.com

MIX
Paper | Supporting
responsible forestry
FSC® C163799
FSC
www.fsc.org

INDEX

26 Grains, 9

7 Bali Spa, 57

7Breaths, 58

Baliga Clinic, 23

Beckenham Place Park Swimming Lake, 40

Bethnal Green Nature Reserve, 33

Blomma Beauty, 14

BODIED, 28

Bonnington Cafe, 37

The British Library, 20

Buddhapadipa Temple, 42

Camden Art Centre, 17

Club Soda, 7

Community Sauna Baths, 29

Conservatory Archives, 24

Daunt Books, 60

Down to Earth, 21

Earl of East, 55

East of Eden, 32

Finnish Church Sauna, 47

Floatworks, 46

Hampstead Heath, 18

Host Cafe, 6

Inhabit, 61

Inner Space, 11

Inner Temple Gardens, 1

Isabella Plantation, 49

Islamic Gardens, Aga Khan Centre, 25

Katsute100, 13

KLORIS, 52

Kyoto Garden, 50

Levitate, 38

London Fields Lido, 27

MASAJ, 8

National Art Library, V&A, 59

National Poetry Library, 43

Neal's Yard Remedies, 12

Old Street Spa Experience, 5

Petersham Nurseries Teahouse, 41

Planetarium, Royal Observatory Greenwich, 45

The Phoenix Garden, 2

Queen's Wood, 19

Re:Mind, 56

Root/25, 36

Ross Nye Stables, 51

Rothko Room, Tate Modern, 44

Sacred Harmony Reiki, 22

Self Space, 53

Shambhala Meditation Centre, 48

She's Lost Control, 35

Soulstice, 15

St Dunstan-in-the-East, 3

St Martin-in-the-Fields, 4

St. Pancras Spa, 26

Studio Pottery London, 54

Tara Yoga Centre, 10

UCHI, 30

Vauxhall Park Lavender Garden, 39

The Well Garden, 34

Wellcome Reading Room, 16

Yoga on the Lane, 31